American Government Today

THE
WHITE HOUSE

LANGUAGE ARTS
SOUTH ST. SCHOOL

By Mark Sanders

P9-CNB-562

STECK-VAUGHN
ELEMENTARY · SECONDARY · ADULT · LIBRARY

A Harcourt Company

www.steck-vaughn.com

Photo Acknowledgments
Cover, p.1: ©PhotoDisc; pp.4, 6, 7 ©AP/Wide World Photos; p.8 ©Cartesia Software; p.11 The White House Collection, courtesy White House Historical Association; p.12 From the collection of Mac G. and Janelle C. Morris; p.15 © Corbis/Digital Stock; pp.17, 18 The White House Collection, courtesy White House Historical Association; p.20 ©PhotoDisc; pp.22, 25, 26 The White House Collection, courtesy White House Historical Association; p.29 The White House; pp.30, 33 The White House Collection, courtesy White House Historical Association; p.35 Culver Pictures; p.36 Brown Brothers; pp.37, 39, 42 ©AP/Wide World Photos; p.44 ©Corbis/Digital Stock.

American Government Today

THE
WHITE
HOUSE

CONTENTS

1600 PENNSYLVANIA AVENUE

One of the most famous addresses in the United States is 1600 Pennsylvania Avenue. In fact, it is one of the best-known addresses in the world. This is the address of the White House in Washington, D.C., where the President of the United States lives and works.

The Capitol is where our laws are made. But inside the White House, decisions are made that affect the lives of all Americans. Many of these decisions also affect people all over the world.

The White House is always in the news. Newspapers and radio and television networks keep reporters in Washington to report what is happening.

South Lawn of the White House

5 ★

President Clinton at a White House press conference

Some of these people only report news from the White House. Almost every day there is something to report— a meeting, a speech, or a press conference.

Every president but George Washington has lived in the White House. Washington helped choose the site, and he approved the design for the building. But the White House was not finished until after Washington left office.

President Abraham Lincoln signed the Emancipation Proclamation in the White House. This document ended slavery in the United States. President Franklin Roosevelt declared war on Japan from there. He also talked to Americans about the war in his famous "fireside chats." These were talks that people heard on their radios. From the White House, President Richard M. Nixon became the first president to resign from office.

Many visitors come every year to tour the home of the presidents. They like to see the large public rooms. They also like visiting the famous gardens. At the White House, visitors learn about the presidents and their families. At the same time they learn about the history of the United States.

Visitors get their tickets to see the inside of the White House.

7

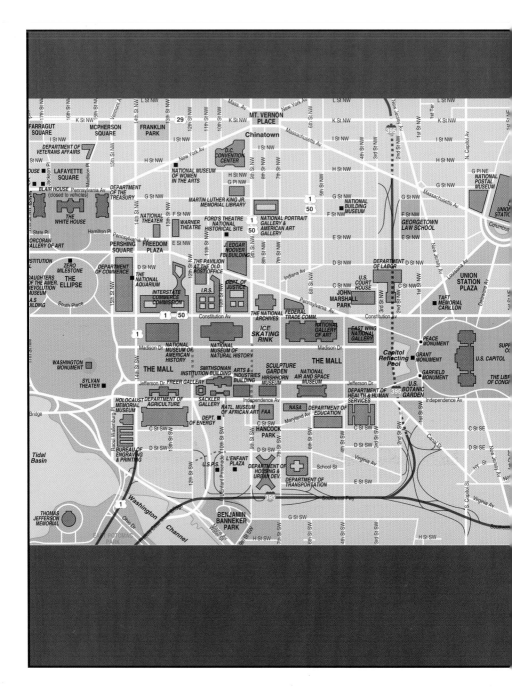

Map of the center of Washington, D. C.

THE HOUSE IS BUILT

George Washington asked Pierre L'Enfant to design
Washington, D.C. This architect decided on a large
Capitol building at one end of the city. About a mile
and a half away, on Pennsylvania Avenue, L'Enfant
wanted to place the new home of the President of the
United States. It was to be large and elegant. At the
same time it would be a comfortable home where the
president's family could live.

In 1791 a contest was held to decide who would
design the new home of the president. The winner was
James Hoban, an architect. Work began, but it wasn't
until 1800 that the first president moved in.

The nation's second president, John Adams, was the
first president to live in the White House. Even when
John and Abigail Adams moved in, there were only six
rooms ready. Legend says that Mrs. Adams hung her
laundry to dry in one of the White House rooms!

9

A view of the White House today, showing all the floors:

A. Ground Floor
  1. East Wing Corridor
  2. Library
  3. Vermeil Room
  4. China Room
  5. Diplomatic Reception Room
  6. Map Room

B. State Room Floor (First floor)
  7. State Dining Room
  8. Red Room
  9. Blue Room
  10. South Portico
  11. Green Room
  12. East Room
  13. Cross Hall
  14. Entrance Hall
  15. Family Dining Room

C. Family Living Quarters (Second floor)
  16. Truman Balcony
  17. Private Living Quarters

D. Third floor
  18. Sunroom
  19. Additional Living Quarters

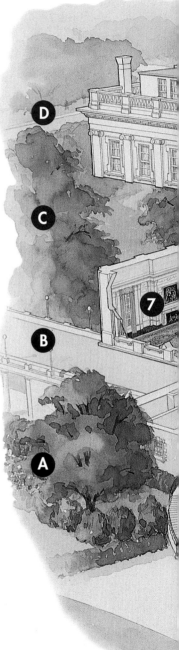

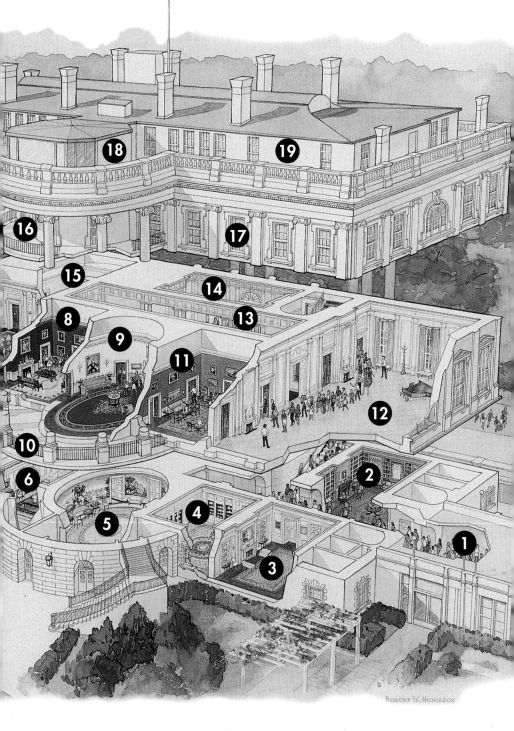

ROBERT W. NICHOLSON

On August 24, 1814, the British attacked Washington, D.C., and set fire to the Capitol. They also invaded the White House. James Madison's wife, Dolley, stayed in the White House as long as she could. Before she left, she rescued a famous painting of George Washington by Gilbert Stuart. She broke the frame and rolled up the picture. By doing this, she saved one of America's early treasures. The British burned the White House, leaving only the outer walls standing.

After the war Hoban returned to restore the building. To cover the smoky outside, the walls were painted white. It was at this time that the words *white house* came into being. It wasn't until the early 1900s that the name became official. In 1902 President Theodore Roosevelt began to use the name White House.

President James Monroe and his wife moved into the White House in 1817. They were the first to live there after the British attack.

The British set fire to the White House in 1814.

CHANGES TO THE WHITE HOUSE

During the 19th century, many plans were made to change the White House. Some thought it was too small. Others felt it was not grand enough.

When Theodore Roosevelt became president in 1902, a large sum of money was put aside to make changes. The West Wing was built, and the president's office was moved there. Also, people wanted the building to look the way it did when it first opened.

In the early 20th century, other changes were made to the White House. A full third floor was added. The West Wing was enlarged, and the East Wing was built. In the 1930s President Franklin Roosevelt built a swimming pool. Roosevelt suffered from polio, and swimming was good physical therapy.

The White House from Pennsylvania Avenue

Many of these changes harmed the building. By the late 1940s, the building was in danger. Large cracks appeared in the plaster. President Harry S Truman's bathtub began to sink through the floor. A piano leg broke through the floor. Something had to be done.

In 1948, while Truman was president, the White House was closed for four years. Major repairs were made to the building. At that time some people wanted to build a new home for the president. But by then the White House stood for the government of the United States. Most people wanted a safe home that would be a reminder of the country's history.

So the inside of the building was torn apart. Pieces of wood were sold as souvenirs. The building was made fireproof. Air conditioning was installed. All this took a lot of money. The cost to taxpayers was about $5.8 million. That was in the 1950s. Today the cost would be about 20 times that amount.

From 1948 to 1952, most of the inside of the White House was completely rebuilt.

In 1952, the Trumans returned to the White House. In addition to being safe once more, most of the building's public rooms looked as they once did.

In 1961 greater attention was paid to the interior. In that year First Lady Jacqueline Kennedy, wife of President John F. Kennedy, founded the White House Historical Association. She searched to find original furnishings. Many of them had been sent away to other places. Things had even been sold or given away over the years. Because of her work, the White House began to look like it used to.

THE OVAL OFFICE

The White House is not just the home of the presidents and their families. It is also an office for the presidents and many of their advisers. In the West Wing is the Oval Office, the president's main working space. It may be the best-known room in the world. The Oval Office has been there since the wing was built in 1902.

Visitors who come to see the president are led into the Oval Office. It is a relatively small room, but it is comfortable. On one side of the president's desk is an American flag. The president's flag stands on the other side of the desk. The presidential seal is in the room's ceiling and carpet. Glass doors lead from the Oval Office into the nearby Rose Garden.

In the West Wing are offices for the vice president, the secretary of state, and the chief of staff. The Cabinet Room is also located there.

The Oval Office is in the West Wing.
The presidential seal is in the carpet.

20

The first lady and her staff have office space on the second floor of the East Wing. On the ground floor level is the Jacqueline B. Kennedy Garden. In good weather visitors are often entertained there.

Many of the president's advisers don't work in the White House. There just isn't enough room. These people work in the Old Executive Office Building near the White House.

The White House from the South Lawn

THE STATE ROOMS

The White House is open to the public every morning except Sundays, Mondays, and holidays. Between 10 A.M. and noon, most of the state rooms may be seen on a tour. More than two million people come to the White House every year.

Inside the South Entrance on the ground floor is the Diplomatic Reception Room. This was once a dark room with water pipes. Jacqueline Kennedy had much to do with making the room more attractive. At one time Franklin Roosevelt delivered his fireside chats from this room. The public cannot see this room or other rooms on the ground floor. These include big kitchens where meals for guests are cooked.

The five state rooms on the first floor of the White House are the best-known rooms in the building. These are the rooms where formal activities often take place. A tour of these rooms begins with the East Room.

The East Room

From the ground floor, visitors climb a large marble staircase to reach the East Room. This is the largest room in the White House. It is the official ballroom and has been since the room was completed in the 1820s. It was in this room that Abigail Adams was said to have hung her laundry.

During the Civil War, Union soldiers lived in this room. After the death, in 1963, of John F. Kennedy people were able to pay their respects to him in the East Room.

The room has also seen happier events. Theodore Roosevelt's children used to roller skate through the East Room. In 1906 Roosevelt's daughter Alice was married in this room. Lynda Bird Johnson chose the East Room for her wedding in 1967.

Guests gather in the East Room before state dinners. Performers who come to entertain the president and guests often appear in this room.

President Millard Fillmore invited the Swedish opera star Jenny Lind to sing in the East Room. But such a huge crowd showed up that she had to sing outside.

The Blue Room

The tour then goes through the Green, Blue, and Red rooms and passes through the State Dining Room on the west side of the house. It ends in the front Entrance Hall.

The Green Room got its name after President James Monroe and his wife hung green curtains in the room. Monroe used it as a game room, where he and his friends played cards. Thomas Jefferson made it his private dining room.

The Blue Room is an oval shape. It is directly above the Diplomatic Reception Room. The Blue Room is used for receptions and small afternoon teas. Martin Van Buren first had this room painted blue, and it has been blue ever since.

The Red Room has been a popular room with many presidents. First Lady Dolley Madison used the room, which was then yellow, for parties. In 1877 Rutherford B. Hayes was sworn in as president in the Red Room.

The State Dining Room was at first much smaller than it is today. When the White House was rebuilt in 1902, it was enlarged. Now the room can seat as many as 140 guests. A portrait of Abraham Lincoln hangs over the fireplace.

The State Dining Room

UPSTAIRS AT THE WHITE HOUSE

The historic rooms on the second floor of the White House are not open to the public. The first family's private quarters on the second and third floors are also closed.

One of the public rooms is the Yellow Oval Room. Before the West Wing was built in 1902, this was the main office for many presidents. Next door is the former Presidential Cabinet Room. This room is now known as the Treaty Room. It is a small room, so only a few people can fit in it.

The Lincoln Bedroom was also once a cabinet room. It was in this room that Abraham Lincoln signed the Emancipation Proclamation in 1863. The room is now used for guests who visit the White House.

The Treaty Room

There are many of Lincoln's belongings in the room. Some say that Lincoln's ghost haunts the bedroom, although Lincoln never actually slept there!

Abraham Lincoln's son Willie died in the Lincoln Bedroom. And Woodrow Wilson recovered in this room from the stroke he suffered while he was president. More happily, Grover Cleveland's daughter was born there.

Across the hall from the Lincoln Bedroom is the Rose Room. It is also known as the Queens' Bedroom. Five queens of foreign countries have stayed in this room, including Queen Elizabeth II of Great Britain.

The rest of the second and third stories are private living quarters for the president's family. These quarters were enlarged during the 1902 changes. There is a sunroom on the third floor that the first family sometimes uses as an extra living room. The sunroom is also known as the solarium. There is a small kitchen off the sunroom where the family can prepare meals.

Today there are 30 rooms and 16 bathrooms in the private quarters. The first families use their own furniture in these rooms.

The Lincoln Bedroom

THE WHITE HOUSE GROUNDS

There are lawns and gardens outside the White House. The well-known Rose Garden is just outside the president's Oval Office. The south side includes a small park for the presidents and their families. This is where the Easter Egg Roll is held each Easter Monday. It is the only day of the year when this park is open to the public.

Dolley Madison began the Easter Egg Roll. At that time it was held in front of the Capitol. Lucy Hayes, the wife of Rutherford B. Hayes, moved the Egg Roll to the White House, where it has been held ever since.

When the president uses a helicopter, it lands on the South Lawn.

A section of the Rose Garden

LIVING AT THE WHITE HOUSE

Presidents have brought different styles of living to the White House. Thomas Jefferson answered the door himself. William Henry Harrison went out with a shopping basket to the nearby markets. When Andrew Jackson was president, the doors were kept open. Anyone could wander in and out. Today security around the White House is very tight.

When the Adamses became the first family, there was no running water in the White House. Servants had to bring water from a nearby well. And there was only an outdoor toilet. A fully equipped bathroom only appeared in the 1880s. President William Howard Taft was so large that he got stuck in the White House bathtub. After that he had an extra-large tub specially built to keep this from happening again. The tub was big enough to hold four people.

Four workers pose in President Taft's extra-large bathtub.

Because the White House is so important, many
new inventions were tried out there. Gas lighting was
introduced in 1848. In 1877 President Hayes asked
Alexander Graham Bell to install a telephone. In 1879
Thomas A. Edison invented the light bulb. The White
House was one of the first homes in the country to have
electricity. Automobiles were first seen at the White
House when Taft was president.

Guests eat Andrew Jackson's giant cheese.

A large tent is set up on the South Lawn.
Today's White House parties are often held outside.

Parties have always been important in White House life. One of the biggest took place when Andrew Jackson became president in 1829. After his inauguration, people rushed to the White House to meet him. People in muddy boots stood on chairs in order to see better. Excited guests broke dishes. A piece of cheese that weighed 1,400 pounds was eaten by noisy guests. Servants soon put tubs of punch on the lawn so people would go outdoors. Jackson himself left through a side door.

FIRST LADIES AND FIRST FAMILIES

The president runs the country, and the first lady runs the White House. She manages the White House staff, which is made up of about a hundred people. They cook, shop, clean, and oversee other workers. The first lady usually hires a social secretary. This person is in charge of all gatherings at the White House. Sometimes as many as 5,000 people will be invited to a social event. And often as many as 200 people will come to a sit-down dinner. Supervising all this takes great skill.

Menus at the White House have depended on the presidents' tastes. Meal planners must be aware of the first family's likes and dislikes. The Eisenhowers liked simple food, served simply. Beginning with the Kennedys, fancier meals were served. This tradition has continued to the present day.

President and Mrs. Clinton welcome children from Washington, D.C., day care centers.

Edith Roosevelt, the wife of Theodore Roosevelt, had her hands full with their six children. They were allowed to go anywhere in the White House. Although the Roosevelt children were noisy, the public loved to read about the fun they had in the White House.

First Lady Lucy Hayes was known as "Lemonade Lucy." She did not serve anything stronger while her husband was in office.

President Woodrow Wilson's second wife, Edith, liked to exercise. She rode her bicycle through White House hallways.

Eleanor Roosevelt was the wife of Franklin D. Roosevelt. She completely changed the role of the first lady. She entertained, as she was expected to. But she also traveled around the country and visited the poor and needy. In addition, she wrote a daily newspaper column. Some people did not approve of Mrs. Roosevelt's role. But many people did, and she was a favorite of the American public.

Not all the presidents have had first ladies. Thomas Jefferson's wife died before he became president. Two of his daughters acted as hostesses. Jefferson also asked Dolley Madison, the wife of his friend James Madison, to welcome people to the White House. James Buchanan was a bachelor. He is the only president who never married.

SPECIAL TIMES AT THE WHITE HOUSE

Christmas is a special time of year at the White House. The lighting of the Christmas tree takes place every year. A large spruce tree is trimmed and put up on the Ellipse. This is a wide section of grass on the South Lawn. A few weeks before Christmas, the first family usually lights the tree. Christmas parties are held for children of White House staff members.

Pets have often made life in the White House interesting. Jefferson kept two bears on the White House lawn. They were a present from members of the Lewis and Clark team. President Benjamin Harrison's son kept a pet goat. During World War I, President Wilson kept sheep on the White House lawn. They trimmed the grass, because the workers had all gone off to fight in the war.

The Clintons' cat, Socks, and a labrador named Buddy were often seen on TV and in the newspapers.

George Bush's wife, Barbara, wrote several books about her dog, Millie.

In 1964 President Lyndon B. Johnson issued an Executive Order to make the White House a museum. The order named a person to take care of the White House and everything in it.

Every four years or every eight years, there is a new president and first family in the White House.

President and Mrs. Bush with Millie on the White House lawn

The family quarters will change each time a new family moves in. But the public part of the White House remains the same year after year. Many of its furnishings have been there for almost 200 years. After all, the White House is there for the nation. It stands for home and family life in the United States.

FACTS ABOUT THE WHITE HOUSE

The White House is 168 feet (51.2 m) long and 85 feet (25.9 m) wide. The building is 70 feet (21.33 m) tall.

The largest room in the White House is the East Room. It is 80 feet (24.3 m) long and 37 feet (11.3 m) wide.

The White House stands on 18 acres (7.3 hectares) of land in the middle of Washington, D.C.

Not counting the office space, the present White House contains 132 rooms. There are five elevators in the White House and one sunroom. There are also a barber shop, a movie theater, and a bowling alley. There are 412 doors, 32 bathrooms, 45 chandeliers, 66 sculptures, and almost 500 paintings.

An aerial view of the White House at night

The ground floor contains an office for the president's doctor. There are a dental clinic, a tailor's shop, a cafeteria, laundry rooms, and carpenters' and painters' shops. There is also a bomb shelter.

It takes 115 people to take care of the White House and the surrounding grounds.

The family quarters measure 5,600 square feet (520 sq m). In the family's quarters there are 30 rooms, 16 bathrooms, and one kitchen. There are 29 fireplaces in the family quarters.

 44

The Presidents

1. George Washington (1789-1797)
2. John Adams (1797-1801)
3. Thomas Jefferson (1801-1809)
4. James Madison (1809-1817)
5. James Monroe (1817-1825)
6. John Quincy Adams (1825-1829)
7. Andrew Jackson (1829-1837)
8. Martin Van Buren (1837-1841)
9. William Henry Harrison (1841)
10. John Tyler (1841-1845)
11. James K. Polk (1845-1849)
12. Zachary Taylor (1849-1850)
13. Millard Fillmore (1850-1853)
14. Franklin Pierce (1853-1857)
15. James Buchanan (1857-1861)
16. Abraham Lincoln (1861-1865)
17. Andrew Johnson (1865-1869)
18. Ulysses S. Grant (1869-1877)
19. Rutherford B. Hayes (1877-1881)
20. James A. Garfield (1881)
21. Chester A. Arthur (1881-1885)
22. Grover Cleveland (1885-1889)
23. Benjamin Harrison (1889-1893)
24. Grover Cleveland (1893-1897)
25. William McKinley (1897-1901)
26. Theodore Roosevelt (1901-1909)
27. William H. Taft (1909-1913)
28. Woodrow Wilson (1913-1921)
29. Warren G. Harding (1921-1923)
30. Calvin Coolidge (1923-1929)
31. Herbert Hoover (1929-1933)
32. Franklin D. Roosevelt (1933-1945)
33. Harry S Truman (1945-1953)
34. Dwight D. Eisenhower (1953-1961)
35. John F. Kennedy (1961-1963)
36. Lyndon B. Johnson (1963-1969)
37. Richard M. Nixon (1969-1974)
38. Gerald Ford (1974-1977)
39. James Carter (1977-1981)
40. Ronald Reagan (1981-1989)
41. George Bush (1989-1993)
42. William Clinton (1993-2001)

Glossary

Advisers Assistants to the president

Architect Someone who designs and plans a building

Ballroom A large room where dances take place

Cabinet A group of advisers to the president. At one time they met in rooms in the main part of the White House.

Declaration A formal statement

Diplomat Someone who is skilled at handling relations between nations

Document An official paper

Inauguration A formal ceremony during which the president takes an oath of office

Presidential seal A design that shows the American eagle. It is used by the president in many places.

Press conference A gathering where something is announced to the public

Reception A social gathering

Restore To take something back to its original form

Solarium A sunroom

State room A formal, usually large, public room

Treaty An agreement, usually in writing

Index

47

American Government Today
THE
WHITE HOUSE

Go behind the scenes in Washington, D.C.,
and discover information about
our government and how it works.

Find out

• How many presidents have lived in the White House

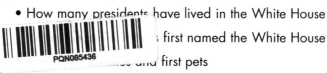 first named the White House

first pets

• About all the important State Rooms and much, more!

Titles in the series

Congress • The Presidency • The Supreme Court
Washington, D.C. • The White House
Your Right to Vote

Steadwell
Books

STECK-VAUGHN
ELEMENTARY · SECONDARY · ADULT · LIBRARY
® A Harcourt Company

ISBN 0-7398-2130-X

90000

9 780739 821305